T0194054

My Life in the US Cold War Army 1956–1958

My View of What Was Happening When
They Said Nothing Was Happening

Second Edition

JERE PROBERT

MY LIFE IN THE US COLD WAR ARMY 1956–1958
MY VIEW OF WHAT WAS HAPPENING WHEN
THEY SAID NOTHING WAS HAPPENING

iUniverse books may be ordered through booksellers or by contacting:

iUniverse
1663 Liberty Drive
Bloomington, IN 47403
www.iuniverse.com
1-800-Authors (1-800-288-4677)

Because of the dynamic nature of the Internet, any web addresses or links contained in this book may have changed since publication and may no longer be valid. The views expressed in this work are solely those of the author and do not necessarily reflect the views of the publisher, and the publisher hereby disclaims any responsibility for them.

Any people depicted in stock imagery provided by Getty Images are models, and such images are being used for illustrative purposes only.
Certain stock imagery © Getty Images.

ISBN: 978-1-5320-7083-9 (sc)
ISBN: 978-1-5320-7084-6 (e)

Library of Congress Control Number: 2019903634

Print information available on the last page.

iUniverse rev. date: 04/11/2019

Contents

Acknowledgments

This work would not have become a reality without the encouragement of my wife, Beverly, and our children, Lisa, Denise, and Stephen. Our longtime friend and neighbor, Dorothy Eckheart, spent many hours editing a narrative that had a severe need to be edited. Without her input, it would not have been completed. Special thanks to Brenda Harrenstein and Jack Cherry for their enthusiastic support of this project.

It has been fun working with every one of you.

Thank you.

★ Setting the Stage ★

One day I had an opportunity to sell a vintage farm tractor at an auction. During the listing process, the auctioneer asked, "What is there about this tractor that makes it special?"

The answer was "It is mine!"

So it is with the following narrative. The only thing unique about this story is that it is mine. Please keep in mind that this account has been composed based on sixty-year-old memories and a few other more-reliable sources. I hope you enjoy it.

I have become more aware with the passage of time that my worldview is a direct result of the environment into which I was born and was raised on a farm in northeast Iowa. By the time I reached ten years of age, my peers and I had been blessed to have known people who were worthy of the word *hero* and were inspiring to the world as it existed. There were neighbor "boys" coming home from years of successful fighting in World War II endangering their lives to keep their loved ones living in freedom. Athletes of great skill didn't see it necessary to brag about how great they were. Women had been serving the war effort at every level. This is just a short list of the many who deserved mention and worthiness of the label of hero. Our hometown of nearly two hundred people had three men survive the Bataan Death March, followed by years in Japanese prison camps, and one person who was a POW in Germany. The able-bodied adults and children I knew were at home working as much as they could. A ten-year-old notices those things.

This jeep was backed over by a beginning driver not the author.

Jumping ahead fifty years, I had an opportunity in the early 1990s to address groups of college students. It was not uncommon for me to ask whether they had heroes. This was followed by my asking them to identify those people they saw in that light. With very few exceptions, that generation listed people in the entertainment business. Rarely did I ever hear a mom, dad, big sister, or brother mentioned as a hero. That is when I began to understand why their generation did not have the same worldview I had. Perhaps this effort will help readers nurture a new view of their homeland.

U. S. GOVERNMENT OPERATOR'S PERMIT DEPARTMENT OF DEFENSE				PERMIT NO. *146*		
NAME OF OPERATOR Probert Jere G				DATE ISSUED 25 Apr 57		EXPIRATION DATE 25 Apr 59
SEX M	RACE Cau	AGE 21	HEIGHT 6'1"	WEIGHT 200	COLOR OF HAIR Black	COLOR OF EYES Brown

The holder of this permit is qualified to operate U. S. Government vehicles and/or equipment specified subject to the restrictions set forth on the reverse hereof.

SIGNATURE OF ISSUING OFFICIAL

TITLE Bn Motor Officer

NAME AND LOCATION OF ISSUING UNIT Hq 3d Bn, 11th Armd Cav Regt APO 225

NOT TRANSFERABLE Permit must be carried at all times when operating Government vehicles.

SIGNATURE OF OPERATOR (Not valid until signed) Jere G Probert

DD FORM 313, 1 AUG 50 REPLACES WD AGO FORM 9-74, 1 AUG 44, WHICH MAY BE USED.

RESTRICTIONS Valid With Glasses Only

QUALIFIED TO OPERATE		
TYPE VEHICLE AND/OR EQUIPMENT	CAPACITY	QUALIFYING OFFICIAL
Sedan	5 Pass	
Truck	1/4 T 1½ Ton	
Truck M38 M37	1/4 T 3/4 Ton	
Truck M35 M135	2½ Ton	
AIV M59	21 Ton	
Tank M41	25 Ton	
Tank M48	50 Ton	

ACCIDENT OR TRAFFIC VIOLATION RECORD		
DATE	NATURE	OFFICIAL

GPO—O—939287   16—62352—1

Maybe an operator's permit will help.

With that background I found myself, in 1956, with two years of higher education and having good health and social freedom (single), so I decided to enlist in the US Army at twenty-one years of age. One

3

of my heroes, Dwight D. "Ike" Eisenhower, was our president. His campaign slogan was "I Like Ike." I liked Ike. I saw active military service as an obligation and nearly inevitable, as did almost every other healthy male of my generation.

I found the process of enlistment in the US Army for a two-year period to be slightly more difficult than I had anticipated. Two years was the standard for a person who was drafted, but three years was the standard for enlistees. After some negotiation with the recruiter, I was able to enlist in the army reserves and apply immediately for two years of active duty. The rest of the package was two years of active reserves and two years of inactive reserves. Ironically, that was the same package a draftee got. The only difference was in the letters in the serial number. The draftee was given a dog tag that started with "US" while mine started with "ER" (for enlisted reserve). There was nothing left but to do it. I signed up, agreeing that on August 13, 1956, I would be in the army. Transportation was provided from our county seat to the state capitol where the swearing-in happened. From there we were loaded on a bus headed for Fort Chaffee, Arkansas. I'd never heard of the place.

Fort Chaffee, originally called Camp Chaffee, was constructed starting September 20, 1941, and completed by Pearl Harbor Day, December 7, 1941. During WWII, some three thousand German POWs were housed there. In the 1970s it provided cover for refugees from the Vietnam War. During the '80s it housed Cuban refugees. Listed in the camp's history under the heading of battles and wars are World War II and the Cold War.

It was a long, hot August ride in an un-air-conditioned bus to Fort Chaffee. My first impression of the place was that it must have been constructed for World War I, if not earlier. The barracks were of two-story wooden frame construction, sitting on rock pillars that stood approximately two feed above the ground level to support the building. I had never seen a building in a climate warm enough so that all the plumbing was in open air under the building.

I had been working on my parents' farm all summer, so the

discipline and the length of workdays were not offensive to me. The first three weeks we were there, the temperature reached 110 degrees Fahrenheit every day. The sheets on the bunks were hotter than my body temperature. As the days passed and we saw someone whose fatigues had been washed, we called them "long-timers." I was one of the few recruits who gained weight during those first eight weeks.

The barracks had wooden floors on both levels. Obviously, in that climate in a building made for the army in 1941, the boards no longer fit together snugly. Every Friday was the day to prepare for Saturday inspection. That involved carrying garbage cans of water in, dumping them on the floors, and mopping. Those of us on the second floor had it much better, even though we carried water up the stairs. When we poured the water on the floor, it ran through the cracks and rained dirty water on the bunks downstairs. They soon found things to cover their beds with on Fridays.

The string of consecutive hot days finally broke. The break came in the form of a rather severe, high-wind thunderstorm. Now, instead of hot, it was hot and wet. I quit worrying about the outdoor plumbing freezing.

I was not bothered by the frequent marches or exercise routines. One exercise I was uncomfortable with was when we had to crawl a significant distance while a .30-caliber machine gun was firing live ammunition just over our backs. I had a cigarette lighter in the front pocket of my new fatigues when I began that crawl, and when I got to the end of it, there was a hole worn through that pocket. They had told us to stay close to the ground. One thing I remember learning during this first eight weeks in the military is that it is humanly possible to make a thirty-gallon US Army galvanized garbage container shine inside and out regardless of its previous condition. Everyone had that opportunity.

We had been strongly warned to not bring cash with us to this training. "After all, you will get paid." They didn't mention payday came at the end of the month. This was during the era when a person could purchase a quarter-pound Baby Ruth candy bar for a quarter of a dollar. When the second or third Sunday at Fort Chaffee came around, I was down to two quarters. On my way to church that day, I bought a candy bar, which I paid for with half my money. During the church service, I dropped the other quarter in the offering. Two days later, I received a letter from my brother with a twenty-dollar bill in it. My faith level greatly increased that day.

Soon we began to worry about advanced training. None of us had been able to sign up for a specific field of training when we entered the service. Rumors were rampant. We did know that we were not all going to the same place for the next phase. It was rumored that an assignment to Fort Collins, Colorado, would mean cold-weather training, which would mean a permanent assignment some place cold. It seemed to be the consensus among everyone with the rank of private that serving the rest of our time at the North or South Pole would not be a preferred option. For me, the powers that be decided Fort Knox, Kentucky, would be my next abode. It was known as the Armor Center, and all I knew about it was that there was supposed to be gold stored in there. We were given a few days to go home before our next assignment. I left Fort Chaffee with my orders (to Fort Knox) in my hand. While at Fort Chaffee, I had developed a fondness for those Baby Ruth candy bars that kept recurring periodically for the rest of my hitch.

I naively expected Fort Knox to be a repeat of Fort Chaffee. I was in for a pleasant surprise. Getting there, however, would not rate as one of my better military experiences. I decided the easiest way to travel from my NE Iowa home to Louisville would be by train from Prairie du Chien, Wisconsin, to Chicago and by air from there to Louisville. The train trip to Chicago proceeded without incident and I was in the depot in a timely manner. I quickly found a travel agency to help book a flight and get me to the airport. All air traffic in the city was grounded because of the weather. "Nothing flying the rest of today" was the answer wherever I asked for help. The personnel at the travel agency went all out to assist me. I did get a little uncomfortable when they began to refer to me as "the potential AWOL" (absent without leave).

The only transportation they could book me on was an all-night "milk train." I discovered that a milk train was one that traveled slowly and seemed to stop at every station, harkening back to the day when they did actually pick up milk. I now had booked a ride whose schedule guaranteed that I would be getting to Louisville after my leave had expired. The orders I had in my hand included a phone number for some outfit. I called the number and got the first sergeant of G Company, Third Battalion, and Eleventh Armored Cavalry Regiment (ACR). He said, "I don't care when you get here, just get here alive." At the very least, that was reassuring.

The author entered the left door and bunked on third floor.

There was a vehicle and two soldiers at the train station in Louisville to meet me. It was the middle of the night when we arrived at the barracks. They showed me where my bed was located, and I was soon sound asleep. Waking up the next day I felt like Rip Van Winkle waking up after his long sleep. The world in which

I awakened in no way resembled the world I left in Arkansas. The building resembled the men's dormitories at one of the better universities in the United States. Instead of leaking board floors, these were highly polished tile. I gave a big sigh of relief upon finding out that the floors were mechanically polished. I wrote my parents that the facility was so nice I felt like an Iowa hog being placed in a finishing pen to fatten up before shipping to a packing plant. In hindsight, that might not have been the correct simile to use in those circumstances. The difference was like moving from poverty to high society in real life.

★ Advanced Training ★

Looks like the correct place!

The first day at Fort Knox, I began to meet men with whom I would eventually make lifelong friendships. At twenty-one years of age, I was considered elderly by the other recruits, many of whom who were eighteen years old. In the bunk next to the one where they placed me was a blond guy from Littleton, Pennsylvania. He was a couple of years older than me and had grown up on a farm. His name was Glenn Hankey. That relationship started that day and has lasted a lifetime. Sixty-two years later, he and I still have a wintertime telephone chats, and I suspect his wife still gives thanks that he and I are separated by a thousand miles.

Glenn Hankey. We saw each other through the rest of the way.

We were to immediately begin training for an exercise named "Gyroscope". Understanding that exercise requires understanding the what, where, when, and why there was a cavalry unit in the US Army in the fall season of the year 1956. Doesn't the very name "cavalry" imply horses with people riding around on them? Not anymore! Cavalry units were from the beginning meant to be reconnaissance outfits, meaning they needed to be highly mobile and, usually, not dragging big weapons or loads that would impair their mobility. From Bible days forward, being mounted on horses was the answer.

In 1956, the cavalry units were still highly mobile and lightly armed. When I arrived, a platoon consisted of a scout squad, which was a couple of jeeps with a .30-caliber machine gun on the jeep and M1 rifles with each man. Next was a mortar squad. They traveled with the mortar in a World War II halftrack vehicle. There was just one of those squads. Each platoon was rounded out with an infantry squad in an M59 armored personnel carrier (APC) with a capacity of ten men.

The APC was powered by two General Motors Corporation (GMC) 305-cubic-inch inline six-cylinder engines. Each engine was attached to an automatic transmission; one powered the left track, and the other one the right track. Synchronizing them so they each shifted at the appropriate moment was an ongoing issue. The platoon was completed with a tank squad that included eight men and two tanks. When I arrived, the tanks were M41s, weighing twenty-five tons. They were powered by Continental six-cylinder (opposed) gasoline engines with five hundred horsepower, an Allison cross-drive transmission, a 76 mm weapon, a .30-caliber and .50-caliber machine gun. In army speak, these were "light" tanks. Ten years after my time with them the Eleventh Cavalry was sent to the Vietnam war, the Eleventh ACR had become airborne by the addition of helicopters.

Each tank crew consisted of a tank commander, a gunner, a loader, and a driver. I had been placed with the tankers upon the night of my arrival. The noncommissioned officer in charge, Sergeant Lewis, decided I was to be the driver of one of the two tanks. The whole unit consisted of men who had just finished the first weeks of basic training, so no previous experience played into where a person was placed. Army protocol at the time said their driver's license gave the driver permission to operate any vehicle smaller than the biggest one on the license. My license included a fifty-ton tank. That permitted me to drive almost any vehicle the army had.

The author posing with someone else's jeep.

My first uncomfortable experience with the military chain of command happened because of that protocol dictating who could drive, accompanied by my first dose of military incompetence revealed when our company pulled guard duty immediately after I was issued the license. G Company was to furnish a jeep and a driver for a motor patrol. At this juncture, the people who should have been driving any of the jeeps in the company had not been issued their driver's license. The motor pool sergeant gave me a jeep and headed me for the guardhouse. Someone from another company was assigned to ride with me on patrol, and we drew the first two-hour shift. I expected two hours on and four off. We drove the streets of Fort Knox at fifteen mph, more or less, as instructed. We came back, parked the jeep, checked in, found our bunks, and went to sleep.

What I did not expect was that the sergeant of the guard, who knew none of the people on duty that night, was going to assign the vehicle for which I had signed and allow other drivers from other outfits to drive it. I was rudely awakened from my self-satisfied sleep early in the morning and confronted by two accusations. One was that I had parked the jeep in a spot that was well marked as belonging to a general, and second, that the dang jeep refused to start for them. Up to that point I had slept well. This all made more sense when I found out other people had been driving and parking the jeep all night. Whoever had driven it last was responsible but apparently untraceable. The outcome was an appointment for me to show up at the general's office later in the morning.

Only in the army for ten weeks or so, and I was already hobnobbing with generals. This was the weekend that my new friend Glenn's wife had chosen to come to visit him. She and Glenn were convinced I was in serious trouble, and I believe I have been reminded of this incident by them each time we met over the next fifty years. Apparently the general was not very impressed with me because he never invited me back. To my ongoing consternation, something very similar to this was going to happen a few more times in the coming months.

When the whole regiment was at full strength, there was in the neighborhood of three thousand personnel involved. With the exception of officers and noncommissioned officers, all other personnel had just finished their first eight weeks of training. By army standards, that was not a very large group. The next step was to prepare everyone and everything for what the United States Army had named Operation Gyroscope.

At the end of WWII, there had been a division of responsibilities agreed upon between the allies in Germany. Berlin was divided as a separate entity, and the rest of Germany was divided between the victors into East and West Germany. The United States ended up with the southern part of what had now become West Germany. England and France also had portions of West Germany, while Russia had East Germany (see map on back cover). One primary border responsibility for the United States was between West Germany and Communist Czechoslovakia. What was going on in terms of military activity was monitored. The migration of people displaced by the traumatic events of the past years was being monitored as well. Much of the illegal immigration of civilians had ceased by 1956. The United States responded to these needs by placing cavalry units along those borders.

Entrance to motor pool Fort Knox—hospital in background.

The Main PX at Fort Knox

A view of the motor pool fuel pumps. When we were in the field, we had 5-gallon pails of fuel trucked to us.

It was right for Fort Knox "The Armor Center" to have a museum named after the WWII armor hero General George S. Patton, Jr.

The attrition of soldiers, as their terms of service ended and they left, meant their units needed to find ways to keep their numbers up. The army's choice was to train a whole new group and replace the old unit with a new group. I have wondered if part of the reasoning was to get the soldiers out of there before they built strong personal relationships with the German nationals. In this instance, the Eleventh Armored Cavalry was leaving Fort Knox heading for Germany, and the Sixth Armored Cavalry was coming home. The fall of 1956 saw advance parties going in both directions. Ostensibly, they were to prepare the way for those yet to make the trip. Everything that was being left behind was being inspected by the ones with the new responsibility. The immediate impact was that the things we were leaving had to meet the approval of the advance party from the Sixth ACR. That meant things like pulling the engine/transmission from a tank so you could clean and paint under it. In this case, some farm boys figured out that if there was water under there and one waited until it froze, paint dumped on the ice looked pretty good.

M41 engine and transmission.

The company commander decided that G Company should have a company Christmas party. It was scheduled to start as soon as things were cleaned up from the evening meal. About ten at night, the officer in charge of the motor pool came to the table where Glenn and I were sitting. Our tank had been moved from our motor pool to the one being used by the Sixth ACR for their inspections several days earlier. The two places were separated by several miles. The officer said our tank had passed inspection and Glenn and I were to bring it back and to do it *now*. He had transportation arranged to get us to where the tank sat. The jeep driver took us to the tank and left us to return the jeep before going back to the Christmas party. Glenn jumped in the tank commander's spot, and I got in the driver's seat. We were about to take off on the streets of Fort Knox with no communication between us—no ground guide either on foot or in a jeep—at ten o'clock on the night of the G Company 1956 Christmas party. We successfully made the trip and parked tank number G37 back where it belonged. Obeying orders, we had violated standing orders concerning driving a single tank on roads or streets without a lead vehicle in front of us. The same was true of parking in the motor pool without a person on the ground guiding the tank. There might have been something wrong with having been at a company party for two or three hours before it all happened. We walked to our barracks thinking we may have done something that had not been done before. Lone tanks driving the streets of Fort Knox at any time was not a sight we had been privy to while we were there.

Installing M41 engine and transmission, winter of 1956.

Winter turned into early spring rapidly. The next step for this Gyroscope thing was to get to the other side of the Atlantic Ocean. We were shipped through rail to the Brooklyn Naval Yard. We were loaded aboard a troop transport late in February or early March.

★ Heading East ★

The author waiting for transportation, Fort Knox to Brooklyn.

Since this is written by an army person being transported in an oceangoing vessel, different parts of the ship will be called things like front and back. The bulk of our company was placed in an area at the lowest level of the ship that had people in it. It also was as far to the back end as it could get. In the center of our assigned area was a large space in the floor containing two doors that opened away from each other. They were huge versions of the cellar doors on the home where I grew up. We were told these doors were opened on each level at the same time so cargo could be loaded to the lowest level. Before we arrived, they closed those doors and covered them with a tarp. All our personal gear was placed on that tarp. The rest of the room was filled with bunks three high. The first hours out were amazingly gentle in the eyes of an Iowa farm boy. Someone said it would be wise to get a top bunk. That turned out to be some of the best advice we had offered to us. Some of the guys started not feeling well as soon as there was movement. By the time we stopped to offload the Harbor Pilot, it was beginning to look like an outbreak of the stomach flu. Most of those soldiers had recently completed a twenty-mile march on Mother Earth but couldn't make it that far in a ship. Two days out, there were two of us left in the company of a hundred or so who were not vomiting. He and I were issued mops and gallon jugs of bleach.

Brooklyn Naval Yards, when everyone
still felt good. March 5, 1957

Each morning for the rest of the trip we mopped and bleached. The navy sent a small group of officers through each morning to inspect our work. We soon discovered that the more bleach we used, the faster the inspectors left. The bleach smell was just too much cleanliness. When we finished our work, we were allowed to take our mops up to the top deck of that thing, tie a rope to the mop, and throw it overboard for as long as we wanted. The salt water cleaned them well. To this day I am still not buying salt from companies that are selling "sea salt."

All aboard the USNS Geiger Transport Ship.

Just as everyone reached the peak of their discomfort, we encountered a North Atlantic spring storm. The two ends of that ship took turns being under water. Those cellar door that went from the bottom of the ship to the top let considerable water come surging down from deck to deck bringing the vomit down to the next deck below and distributing it on the men's duffel bags which were placed on those doors. There were ladder wells that reached from deck to deck. A ladder well reminded me a lot of the chutes that are on vertical silos where silage is/was stored on farms. The difference was that our silos stood still.

A quiet day with no land in sight.

By this time the ship was diving into the water until, in my opinion, too much of the front of the ship disappeared. At this point the propeller that pushed the ship was lifted out of the water. As it lifted out of the water, the vibration in our space at the bottom and back of the ship was incredible. It was caused by the last few feet of the propeller banging the water rather than running in the water smoothly. When the front of the ship decided to come back up, the vibration repeated as violently as it had when going the other direction. During this storm, the only guys allowed on the top deck were those of us with mops. To go up or down, we had to use those ladders in the ladder wells. They did have something of a protective enclosure around them. When your end of the ship was going up, you hung on for dear life. When your end was going down, you could let go of everything. Then you and the mop seemed to stay suspended in place while the ladder whizzed downward past you. There came a moment of equilibrium when it was time to grab the mop and the ladder steps, and be prepared for the next trip up.

A small army band met us when we disembarked at Bremerhaven, Germany. We once again loaded on a train. This one was headed for Regensburg, a city of about a hundred thousand people. Regensburg is in Bavaria about sixty miles north of Munich. Only the Third Battalion was headed there. The First, Second, and Headquarters Battalions were stationed in other cities. We were located in what had been a WWII German Army facility now relabeled Fort Skelly. The Danube and two other rivers came together downtown. Fort Skelly was easy walking distance from downtown. Compared to the previous places I had been stationed, Fort Chaffee or Fort Knox, Fort Skelly was hardly a speck on a map. Most of our training would be done in what were historic German Army training areas.

Main gate to Fort Skelly; Regensburg in the background.

As we settled in our new home, the driver's license experience in Fort Knox was repeated with some variations. Some of the equipment left for us by the previous occupants was quite dysfunctional. The first things to show up in need of replacement were six jeeps that could barely propel themselves. The Third Battalion mechanics were not equipped to perform the needed maintenance. It was decided that the jeeps should be driven to the regimental motor pool located in Straubing for inspection, and then driven to Dachau to Seventh Corp, where they would be swapped out for rebuilt models. Just as it had happened in Kentucky, driver's licenses became an issue. They had six jeeps that needed drivers and only five qualified drivers. I was the only one they could find with a driver's license to give them the needed six drivers. This mess existed because, according to the army, the licenses we received in the United States a few months earlier needed to be replaced by licenses issued in Germany.

In charge of this escapade was a Second Lieutenant Johnson, whom I had never met. He had the vehicles tested and ranked the jeeps one through six based on their condition, with sixth being the worst of six very ill jeeps. He then had them travel in a convoy with the best jeep leading. There is a phenomenon we called "accordioning" that happens in a convoy. The space between each vehicle tends to get bigger as the convoy travels. Every mile they travel increases the distance each one has to make up. This is especially true with inexperienced drivers. When it reaches an inappropriate distance, the drivers begin to close up and the last vehicle has a huge job of catching up to do.

Lieutenant Johnson had given me vehicle number six, the last one in line. Trouble was visible on the horizon when we left the main gate at Skelly. Lieutenant Johnson, with his driver and his perfectly healthy jeep, were at the gate. He was standing waving each vehicle through the gate, including the one he was supposed to be riding in. I was supposed to be last. He was supposed to jump in his jeep, and they would pass everyone and be the leaders. His driver and jeep did pass everyone, but the driver didn't have his cargo; the lieutenant was still standing at the gate. He had neglected to take himself along. About an hour later, a civilian car passed all of us with Lieutenant Johnson in the passenger seat.

A typical scene in rural Germany.

The day after the inspection, we headed for Dachau. Lieutenant Johnson led the way. We drivers were not given maps or written instructions but were told, rather in passing, the highway numbers we would be using. A couple of hours later I, with my lame duck jeep, was surviving the accordion impact very well. We were usually within sight of the one ahead of us.

We finally came to the outskirts of a small city. The jeep ahead of me had a driver and passenger. They stopped along the road and proceeded to urinate. When they finished, they jumped in the jeep and pulled out of there like a drag race. There I was with no vehicle in sight. I proceeded into this city that looked much like it must have looked two hundred years ago. It had crooked, narrow, hilly streets, but not a jeep to be found. It might have helped if I could have spoken German. The good news was that I remembered the road numbers that were to take us to our destination. I found myself on the correct road on the correct side of town.

I had successfully traversed the city; I was rural again, but I had not found any jeeps. Confident that I was where I needed to be, I thought that I must have been traveling so slowly that they were out of sight ahead of me. I decided I would drive fifteen more minutes as fast as the lame jeep could go. If I didn't catch them, I would come back, park on the edge of town, and let them find me. Ten minutes into this plan, I came upon a German farmer by the road. With a little waving of hands, I was able to determine from him that no other jeeps had passed this way. I knew either there were no jeeps going past his place or there were nine jeeps because he kept saying "nine."

Not a good place to be lost and alone.

I turned around and headed back to town. When I arrived back at the edge of town, there were the other five jeeps parked with Officer Johnson and his jeep. He immediately began to scold me for messing up his plan. It turned out that he had gotten lost and led the convoy around downtown for forty-five minutes. I had driven through town while he was lost in it. The incompetence had just begun. We did proceed unimpeded to Dachau. We arrived in the late evening. Upon arrival we found that Lieutenant Johnson had made no arrangements for our overnight stay or for our meals. We didn't eat. Someone found us blankets and bed frames without mattresses to use. I regret we were not able to explore any of the history of one of Hitler's infamous institutions. Dachau was one of his killing camps where people, mostly of Jewish ethnicity, were slaughtered. Compared to the trip down, the trip back to Regensburg in a good running jeeps was fun. The sad part of this account is that later in the year, Lieutenant Johnson was killed in a highway collision while driving a civilian vehicle.

A New Home

★   ★

Guardhouse on left, battalion headquarters on right: Fort Skelly.

Parade field and barracks.

The Fort Skelly barracks in which we were now housed were comfortable, though different from anything I had experienced up to this point. We were assigned squad rooms that held six to eight men. The lower five feet of the walls were painted and the upper part whitewashed. Each of us had a footlocker and a wall locker. On top of the wall locker was our tanker roll, which was a version of a backpack that contained enough items to last in the field for a prolonged period of time. When an alert was sounded, we were expected to be at the tank with that pack within minutes. Alerts were a frequent occurrence and often required us to move out on a maneuver. Sometimes we would be gone a couple of weeks, but more commonly it was a few days. There was a German handyman who hung out around the barracks and did handyman chores. He was a good resource. He understood the US Army, and he knew the community.

The squad room at its worst.

Glenn and the author writing home.

The four men on each tank crew were expected to qualify with all the weapons on board the tank. The tank itself, as previously mentioned, carried a 76 mm gun and a .50-caliber and .30-caliber machine gun. The driver was issued a .45-caliber pistol, which meant I had to qualify with it as well as the bigger stuff. The .45 was a qualifying nightmare to me. I had trouble even hitting the target, to say nothing about getting enough points to qualify. On my first trip to the firing range, I tried to convince the trainer that the sights were bad. His response was firing an expert rating with my .45. I made arrangements to come back the next week to try again. The next week I scored my worst score ever. The instructor, rather than accept the fact that he couldn't teach me, qualified me and told me not to come back. I think he meant forever. I easily qualified with the 76 mm main tank gun and the two machine guns.

Content of tankers rolls on top of wall lockers.

Going to the firing range to qualify with the 76 mm main gun, while not a big challenge as far as qualifying, did have some bumps in it. First, we were not the only tank on the firing line. There might be as high as twenty of them on the line. They were not very far apart. We were given no ear protection. These guns had a "blast deflector," which seemed to deflect the sound ninety degrees in either direction. If a person was standing in the wrong place during firing, it caused extreme pain in the ears.

At that time, the army expectancy was what they called 100 percent second-round hits or kills. This was to be accomplished by watching through the sight where the first round hit and moving that place on the sight to the center of the target. The crosshairs were pretty much out of the picture for the second round. When we did this in Germany, the tanks were left on the firing line overnight. At the close of the first day, every unit was issued a cleaning cloth to clean the bore of the gun. In typical army fashion, there was never enough. When they came with trucks to haul us back to the base, Sergeant Lewis told me to stay on site when they all left, pick up all the rags that were left on the ground, and store them in our tank. He would send someone out to pick me up. I didn't relish riding in the back of a truck, anyway. I had just gotten a good start on this somewhat questionable project when a jeep pulled on site. It had a driver, an enlisted man, and an officer. Turns out they were posting the first guard of the evening. The officer asked me what I was doing as soon as they saw me with my arms full of rags. I responded with words that would work every time: "Just policing the area, sir." His response was "Carry on." Because we had picked up the rags, when it came time to clean up after firing, we had an abundance of material with which to do the job.

The second incident on the firing line had potential of a disaster. The tanks of that era, when combat ready, carried a rather large number of rounds of ammunition. Normally the ammo was at the Fort Skelly base, under lock and key in the ammo dump. There were two storage areas in the turret. There was the large area that held most of the ammo but was more difficult for the loader to access, and there was the ready rack, which held about eighteen rounds and was easily accessed.

Lined up in motor pool mud.

There is always a protocol, and loading ammo from the ground to the racks is no exception. Three people were involved in the loading process. The first commandment was that when handling a round, there was always one hand covering the primer and the other one around the ogive (pointy end). The second commandment was to always transfer it to the next person with the ogive pointed down; and third, don't release a round until you are certain the next person has it. This day the ammo people had delivered enough for the day's exercise and placed it on the ground beside the tank. Our tank commander that day was Sergeant Lewis, who liked to say he had helped write the book on these tanks. He was not bragging much; he was very knowledgeable on M41s and M48s. He placed me in the turret to load the rounds in the racks. He stood on the sponson boxes which were like fenders over the tracks. Glenn and Ted were on the ground handing the rounds up to Sergeant Lewis, he was handing them down through the open hatch to me, and I was putting them in the racks. Following protocol again, I loaded the ready-rack first. After we had handled the first eighteen rounds, we had a rhythm established.

Front, left to right, Harold Conley, tank commander; Glenn Hankey, gunner; Ted Van Delden. *Center rear,* Jere Probert, driver.

Driver's compartment, M48 tank.

When I had to take the next round to the other site, it broke the rhythm, and Sergeant Lewis broke the protocol on releasing the round he was delivering to me. I had not made it back to the open hatch when he dropped his round six feet from the top of the turret to the steel deck. It seemed like an eternity before I corralled that round. It really bounced around in there because it landed on that pointy end. All four of us knew what had happened, but there was absolute silence until I called for the next round. I was remembering the training on this; the trainer said that it takes fifteen pounds per square inch of pressure to activate the primer. Then he said, "That is exactly what it takes to bite through a Jelly bean." At least four of us, or maybe more, were blessed that day and didn't know what a blessing it was to have avoided the possibility of exploding forty 90 mm rounds.

Steering wheel, M48 tank.

Every two years there was a training that we called a "war game". Seventh Army was divided into a Red Army and a Blue Army, and we spent two weeks chasing each other around the countryside. Hohenfels and Grafenwoehr are two of the training areas in Germany that we used. They date back to at least the First World War. There were still stables left as they had been ready to have horses living there again. We had deployment there for our gunnery and live-fire training. Some of this became more realistic than I would have liked. There were fighter planes involved. I think they were shooting films where bullets would have gone. There were times when they flew in closer than I thought they needed to.

One evening we (our army) were settled in on the top of a large hill. We were set up in a perimeter defense, meaning there were guards all the way around the area. We had been out several days, and army kitchens had a way of getting lost—especially if their route took them by a *gasthaus*. In English that would be tavern. We had left for this exercise with some purchased food in the sponson boxes of the tank. That supply was getting small and old. As it started to get dark, a light appeared east of us across a large valley. Sergeant Lewis "suggested" that the loader on our tank and I go to that light and see if we could come up with something better than WWII C-rations to eat.

Ted Van Delden.

Our loader was about my age and of Holland Dutch-Jewish extraction. His name was Theodora (Ted) Van Delden. Before he was drafted, Ted was an employee of Royal Dutch Airlines (KLM). This was well before the book about Ann Frank hit the market, but his account of his life sounded identical to hers. He had come to the United States after the war, grew up, and ended up a soldier. Ted was the first person I met who was a professing homosexual. It is interesting that none of his comrades cared what his sexual preference was. What qualified Ted to be on this current food-hunting adventure was that he spoke six different languages. He seemed like a good choice to me as well.

We had to sneak through the posted guards to make this walk. It was farther to the light than was anticipated. When we arrived at the light, we found one man. He was cordial and invited us in. Ted talked him into selling us some bread and a dozen hard-boiled eggs. Those were the only hard-boiled eggs I saw in the service. We headed back to where we thought we came from. There was no light to guide our return trip, but we made it easily and worked our way through the perimeter defense without incident.

There was another "food happening" shortly after that one. This time none of the other units were with us. A German national approached us and invited the crew to his home for a noon meal. When I got there, the other guys were eating. This farmer had butchered a mature male hog, fixed it like soup, and served it. The smell and the presentation of this meal made me realize I was not as hungry as I thought. This time I did excuse myself and ate the C-ration.

I was not prepared for other cultural differences we were about to experience. I was taken by surprise when May 1, 1957, came around, and we were restricted to base because May 1 is a Communist holiday—World Wide Worker's Day—and there were dangers for American service people on the streets of Germany. After Russia launched the first artificial satellite and called it *Sputnik* on October 4, 1957, it was common to meet a German adult on the street and have him say "beep, beep, beep," mimicking the radio impulses Sputnik was sending back to earth, and then walk away with a giggle. They were more aware of the political ramifications than we were.

A real Dutch windmill.

After we were settled in the Regensburg Barracks and had begun to increase the perimeter of our relationships, I was approached by another midwestern farmer. He was married, a confessing Christian from Scotts Bluff, Nebraska. His name was Alvin Asa. He suggested we take a vacation together. We were able to get simultaneous ten-day leaves. We headed north for Amsterdam via rail and only made a few short stops along the route. When we exited the train in Amsterdam, there was an immediate and new atmosphere for a US soldier in uniform. We were treated almost like we were some sort of royalty on a state visit. The feeling was as if they actually liked us, wanted us to be pleased with them, and to enjoy every visit. This was in sharp contrast with any German national's presentation. My traveling companion noticed this too. We talked about it and decided it was about who won WWII. While there, we had private tours of what made Holland famous: windmills, canals, acres and acres of beautiful flowers in fields, big flower auctions, and silent auctions like we had never seen before. We also saw how to make wooden shoes.

Upon our return to our outfit, I talked about this with Ted Van Delden, the Dutch immigrant who had lived an Anne Frank's life hidden in an attic because he was a Jew. I told him how impressed Alvin and I were with our welcome in Holland and asked if we were wrong in our first impressions. We asked him to explain.

He said, "You can't understand what it is like to hide in an attic or be hidden by someone who was risking his life to do it." He went on to say, "Or you can't know what it is to not have had enough food for most of the last ten years, and suddenly see big airplanes with a big US star on the wings and people dumping lots of food out the back of the plane. Dumping it out for you! You are right; the Dutch people won't soon forget what Americans did."

This conversation took place during a brief stop at our barracks to drop off and pick up laundry before finishing our leave. The next phase of our schedule included a trip to Munich, where Hitler had thrived, and into the German Alps, where he had used slave POW labor to build a fantastic lodge for himself. Strange how one short visit with a person named Ted from Holland changed our view of what we were about to see.

★ More Training ★

Playing in the mud.

One of the trainings found us being chased by another tank. This was on a narrow road, and we were way ahead of him when we came to a village. The first buildings we came to had rock walls. They were directly across the narrow road from each other. I slowed the tank to a crawl and stopped just as the tracks hit the sides both buildings. The tank commander surveyed the scene and said, "Drive her through. You are only taking about an inch of rock off each one." I always wondered if there was anyone in the buildings at the time.

On some occasions, when we were going on exercises, we moved as a unit on their highways. They never let us on the Autobahn. We did get on other hard-surface roads, and it was often an interesting and fun way to move. Macho German automobile drivers enjoyed playing chicken with a twenty-five or fifty-ton tank that was approaching them on the highway at twenty miles per hour or so. They would intentionally get across the centerline and then smile and wave when the tank moved out on the shoulder to miss them. I noticed that if we didn't move away from them they could, and they would, get back on their side of the highway unscathed. Our tank commander said during one of these journeys, "I'm getting tired of seeing Volkswagens disappear beside the tank." His point of view was from on top of and in the center of the tank, and it looked as if we were running over them. It was infrequent that two of those drivers in a row played that game. There had to be a moment of panic when the driver of the car realized the tank wasn't going to be forced to move over.

Obsolete tank monument at Vileseck, Germany
Tank Training Center, January 11 – 27, 1958.

When I arrived in Fort Knox with the Eleventh ACR, they were equipped with M41 light tanks, known as "Walker Bulldog" tanks. I never heard them called Walkers or Bulldogs. They were fast, agile, and had "T-bar" steering that looked like bicycle handlebars in front of the driver. After our arrival in Germany, these were replaced with M48 "Battle" tanks. The M48s were the third tank model known as the "Patton." It is steered with a small, almost-round steering wheel rather than a T-bar. I never heard one of them called a Patton by a military person. Both of these tanks had torsion bar suspension which resulted in an extremely smooth, comfortable ride.

When the M41 light tank had the 76 mm tank gun locked in the travel lock position, it was not pointing straight back from the turret. It was angled back toward the left side of the tank.

The 1958 War Game took place in February. It was called Operation "Sabre Hawk". The pictured track vehicles are waiting at the railhead to load and move out.

Because of this design, if while on a highway the tank made a sharp right turn, the muzzle would protrude over into the other lane of traffic. This rarely happened. The protocol when traveling on the highway was that there would always be a jeep leading the convoy.

If the tank was being driven in other noncombat situations, there was to be a soldier who acted as a ground guide using hand signals to direct the driver.

On one of our outings, we were being led by an officer in a jeep. He decided it was break time and stopped the jeep. Doing exactly what the protocol demanded, he dismounted and assumed the correct position to ground guide. His intention was for the tanks to pull off on the right-hand shoulder out of the way of traffic on our lane. He signaled a hard-right turn, which I performed. Neither the officer nor I could know that, exactly at that moment, a German truck was going to attempt to pass us. Since we were the lead tank at the time, the truck had already safely passed all the rest of the vehicles. Unfortunately, these separate circumstances resulted in the 76 mm gun tube entering the cab of the passing truck through the passenger side window. The cab of the truck stopped immediately upon impact, but the rest of the truck briefly continued on. No one was injured, but it seemed like a good idea to stay in the tank during our break. German police and military police were soon on the scene working out the details. There were many German words spewing forth from the truck driver. One can only wonder how he explained that incident to his boss.

An M48 on a German street.

As I was drawing near to the end of my tour, and after I had been driving tanks for nearly eighteen months and would be leaving the outfit in a couple of months, they sent me to tank driver's training. There were four of us sent; two were sergeants from another company, one was a private from our infantry squad, and me. We were assigned to one tank as a crew. There were about twenty-five tanks involved in this exercise. The training was in one of the camps in Bavaria in early spring.

It was not uncommon to experience a heavy, wet snowstorm in Bavaria. This was a day when one of those storms arrived. I was the driver that day for the trip to the training area. The training area was large enough to provide space for all tanks to function at the same time. The two sergeants left the other two of us in a shelter for the rest of the day and proceeded to take turns playing with the tank. It must have snowed nearly a foot that day. When it was time to return to base, we were to be the last tank in line and I was returned to the driver's position. The road, or trail, into this site made its way across a rather deep, wide, and steep ravine. There was a trail carved into both sides of the ravine.

An M48 with required ground guide in motor pool.

The trail went down lengthwise of the ravine, crossing from one side to the other at the bottom. The trail was perhaps thirty feet wide on both banks of the ravine and reversed itself at the bottom to proceed up the other side. Both top ends of that trail had a ninety-degree turn leading into flatter terrain on higher ground. We were running M48s that day. Weighing in at fifty tons, they were considered a battle tank. They had a 750-horsepower gasoline engine and an Allison cross-drive transmission. This combination performed very well and had some characteristics of a Buick of the era. For example, the transmission gave one the impression that it was all hydraulic without any gears. The shift sequence was also similar to a Buick. It went from park to neutral, to low, to high, to reverse. The tank steered and accelerated more quickly in low. In high, the steering moderated noticeably. If one thinks of traveling thirty miles per hour, then unintentionally completely stopping one track in an effort to negotiate a turn, it becomes understandable why the steering was made more gentle at higher speeds. The tracks had large, hard rubber pads secured to them to enable travel on hard surface roads without damaging the road.

Because we were the lead tank going out, we were to be the last tank leaving the area for the trip back. When we moved out of the ninety-degree turn to head down the long, steep incline to the bottom of the ravine, we were presented with a trail lined with fifty-ton tanks sitting on packed, slippery, wet snow. They were alternated one on the left side of the trail and the next on the other side. When the deep, wet snow was run over by the hard rubber tracks, it had become like wet ice. This was a time I was glad I had learned to drive things in the icy, slippery midwestern United States. I was also thankful I knew how the transmission worked.

Getting lined up to move out.

Someone had spun to a stop going up to the far side of the ravine, causing emergency stops going up that side and those going down the other. My first reaction upon seeing this was to shift into low gear to improve braking and steering and not lose control. For a moment, I felt like we were the fifty-ton moving part in a pinball machine with equal-size pins to bounce off of. We missed the first parked tank. Going the rest of the way down, I left the engine at idle to keep better handling ability. Soon we were at what looked like a 180-degree turn that headed us uphill on the other side of the ravine. Just as we started up, I shifted into high and floor-boarded it. At full speed the engine screamed, but it was not going to spin out with the transmission in high. Steering became a little trickier, but it could be done. When we approached the lead tank, which was nearly to the top and the first tank to spin out, the training officers who were in the jeep leading the group were now all out of the jeep acting like cheerleaders. They waved us on with no one in front of us.

We drove to the motor pool without incident, washed the tank, and ate our evening meal before the next crew came in. Our intercom on the tank had been completely silent through the whole experience. No orders or directions had been issued. Both of the sergeants had been riding in the tank with their torsos above the hatches on the top of the turret. One of them was in the tank commander position, and the other was just observing. When we had dismounted, the sergeant who was riding in the tank commander position said to the other sergeant, "Have you ever seen such a (expletive deleted) job of tank commanding in your life?"

The second sergeant responded "You never said a word on the whole xxxx trip." I thought that must have been the army's version of a compliment for me.

The internal environment in these tanks was functional without being uncomfortable. With a little practice, I was able to eat salted in-the-shell peanuts while driving a 50-ton tank. Each crew member had an assigned area containing enough space to be comfortable. Only the gunner could not easily access the outside. However, it was not unusual to hear a tanker say, "If World War III happens, I'm deserting to the infantry." We were riding around in a huge steel container packing two hundred gallons of gasoline giving the tank the potential of becoming a gigantic oven. Russia capitalized on that potential with something called a "molotov cocktail". It was just a matter of throwing a breakable container with a small amount of gasoline on the engine compartment of an enemy tank to set it on fire.

During the time I was involved in refueling tanks, fuel was handled in five-gallon cans delivered in trucks and handled by hand. Our best gas mileage was in the neighborhood of two gallons per mile.

Every tank crew was required to pass a proficiency test. Our crew was scheduled for the test during the summer of 1958. This test was taken after I left. It was called the "tank crew proficiency test", and in tanker jargon became "the TCPT." That test was run with all hatches closed and using live ammunition. The only view outside was the use of vision blocks, which were simply mirrors arranged in a way that gave a view up and out.

The person functioning as ground guide in the picture (captioned "Ground guide stopping tank on flatcar. His head looks in danger!") of a tank loaded on a railcar was Sergeant Conley. His first name was Harold. There was nothing macho about Sergeant Conley; John Wayne, the movie star from years past, would have loved to have starred in a movie playing the part of the real-life Conley. He started life in Manhattan, Kansas, and by the time I met him, he had seventeen years in the army. He was a veteran of the African Campaign, the invasion of Normandy, and the Korean War and had been a prisoner of war during WWII. He had earned three Purple Hearts during his years of service. It was not unusual to meet WWII veterans still in the service twelve years after the war, but it was rare to meet one with a record like his. For his own private reasons, he refused to wear any of the ribbons he had earned.

★ Life in the Field ★

Loading tanks on flatcars. Note the number
of cars that were traversed.

Transporting by rail was not always as easy as it sounds. The size and weight of the tanks involved created its own problems. In a normal situation, ten flatcars were backed into a loading dock, and the tanks were driven off the dock onto the first car and then proceeded car to car to the last vacant car. The immediate issue was that the M48 tank had an overall track width about eighteen inches wider than the deck of the car it was being driven on. That meant about nine inches of the track was hanging off each side of the rail car. The German railroad people were particular about those measurements. I guess it had something to do with going through tunnels.

Yard worker centering tank on car.

Ground guide stopping tank on flatcar.
His head looks in danger!

The second issue was the weight of the tank. The weight was a potential problem when driving off the car the tank was on and getting safely onto the next one. The railroad cars had springs at both ends. When the tank was centered on the car, the springs were more than adequate. As the tank was driven toward the next car, the springs on the end of the first car began to depress. As the loading began, the lowering of the first car did not impact the second car, so it stayed at its original height. As the tank continued to move, the front of the tank would begin to climb onto the second car. That process threw the center of gravity even farther back, causing the first springs to continue to compress even more, which aggravated the incline even more. The tank continued forward until there was more weight above the second car than the weight compressing the first springs. At that point the springs that had fifty tons of pressure on them released the stored-up energy like a bow shooting an arrow.

The rear of the tank shot up, and the front went down like a ship in a storm. Everyone breathed a sigh of relief when the tank settled in a stable position. The process was repeated until the last car in line had a tank on it, and the next tank repeated the process. If the tank did not end up centered left to right on the car, it could take a little time to move it sideways when it was already hanging off both sides. After making the German train people happy with its position, triangular wooden blocks were placed in front and behind each track and spiked to the wooden floor of the car. This was followed by chains and a chain binder front and rear.

We were returning by rail from a two-week exercise. All the tracked vehicles were on the train. All the crews were in a passenger car that was not nearly big enough. It was night, the seats were full of sleepers, and those of us left over found a space in the aisles, on the luggage, or at the feet of others. Regardless of conditions, we all quickly went to sleep. The train stopped, and no one noticed until a couple of men in German railroad dress showed up in our car. One of the flatcars had developed what my father used to call a "hot box" (a.k.a. a failed bearing between one of the railroad flatcar's wheels and the axle upon which it was mounted).

The failure happened to be on the car carrying our tank. They told us the train crew had another car backed up to ours, and if we could off-load our tank and have it on the other car in fifteen minutes, we would head out. If we did not accomplish that, we (the crew) and the tank would be left wherever we were until arrangements could be made to get us hooked to another train. There were four grown-up tankers thinking, *I just want to go home.* Home meant someplace where we would be able to eat and sleep. With light from flashlights, the task was completed within the time constraints. The two German train men pitched in to help us make it work.

A field expediency shelter.

In some ways, German agriculture looked primitive in the mid-1950s. A team of cows pulling a wagonload of manure, or a cow and horse hitched together, was not unusual. There seemed to be frequent rain or snow that forced many people to wear rubber knee boots. That wet weather also made living in the field uncomfortable for soldiers. One of the creative ways the German farmers compensated for the wet environment was "cocking" their hay after it was cut. They cut three sticks of wood about two inches in diameter and eight to ten feet long. They tied them together on one end and placed the other ends far enough apart to look like the frame for a Native American tepee. They then stacked the hay around them and over them. The structure would shed some of the rain; and when it was a drying day, it exposed the hay to the drying weather.

All that is needed is a Baby Ruth candy bar. No self-respecting Boy Scout would camp in this swamp. We'd been here two days. February 1958.

Every tank carried a rather large tarp that could be used to protect the tank from the weather. The tank also carried a long piece of inch-and-a-half or two-inch pipe used to clean the gun tube. Each member of the crew carried one shelter half—which could be attached to one carried by someone else—to make a little two-man tent. Some members of our tank crew figured out a scheme that involved borrowing those sticks the farmers cocked hay on, fastening the piece of pipe to them, pulling the large tarp over the pipe, and having a very usable instant four-man tent. Then we could use the shelter half to lay our bedroll on giving us a much dryer sleeping arrangement.

Three infantrymen warming up over a 750 hp gas engine.

Our stated purpose for being in Germany in the first place was to provide border security between West Germany and Communist Czechoslovakia. That duty was periodic; we were only on the border one month at a time, and then the next unit would take over and we would go back to Fort Skelly in Regensburg where there was always company guard duty. We called this "pulling guard". There were several different guards posted each night. All but one of the posts were two hours on and four off. Only two shifts were served by each person each night. The practice on those posts was for the guard to work at the motor pool all day, go on guard, do his eight or twelve hours, and work again the next day. The one post that was twenty-four hours was for the ammunition dump. That was two hours on and four off for twenty-four hours. This was also the only post that required the guard to carry live ammo and the only one I always requested because I found this post the easiest to perform. As a tank driver, my assigned weapon was a .45-caliber pistol. That is the same one I couldn't hit anything with at the firing range.

Tired and dirty!

While on guard, I was given a clip of ammo but wisely never put it in the weapon. I thought this arrangement to be much more reasonable than carrying around a heavy old M1 rifle the way the infantry guys had to do. We were issued a shoulder holster for carrying the pistol. Hip holsters were not acceptable. The weapons and equipment for each company were under lock and key in that company and were to be signed out by the person to whom they were originally issued. They were inspected by the officer of the guard as part of the "mounting of the guard."

One of these guard days provided another opportunity for me to find myself at odds with a person carrying a lot more rank than me. When we signed out a weapon, we always got the same one. It was "mine." Holsters were more loosely supervised. You just took one that was on the counter. As I was getting ready for guard one day, I spotted a beautifully finished holster and asked for it. It looked great for inspection. The next day, after finishing guard duty, I was rather privately informed that the captain in charge of G Company had to be in a parade yesterday and couldn't find his holster. They never figured out how that holster could be gone one day and be back in the correct place the next day. From that day forward, I made sure I wore any holster but that one.

Pulling guard didn't happen often and could be a good break from the boring routine of day-to-day activities. If there was any change in this procedure, the word quickly passed through the ranks. In the business world this internal passing of information is often called the internal communication system. The word was out that a new sergeant had come to Eleventh ACR, Third Battalion, and when he pulled sergeant of the guard he liked to sneak up on a posted guard and find him not doing what he should have been doing. My next time on guard, that sergeant was on duty. I was able to get the ammo dump post too. The guardhouse was positioned diagonally all the way across Fort Skelly from the ammo dump in our comparatively small camp. The barracks, the officer quarters, and married housing separated the ammo dump from the guardhouse. Since I didn't allow myself one round of ammo (like Deputy Barney Fife was allowed to have on the Andy Griffith show), I thought I might need to have a plan. I'll explain a little about how the .45-caliber pistol works. The .45 has a slide that must be pulled all the way back and released to load a round into the firing chamber. When that is done in the middle of a dark summer night, it can be heard from a long distance, and there is no question about what you just heard. What the hearer on this day didn't know was that there was no clip holding ammo to go with the sound.

In the middle of the night, I saw a shadow moving between the married housing buildings. I deduced that was the sergeant of the guard stalking me, or there was some hanky-panky going on in the married section. I stayed in the deepest shadows I could find, and when he stopped by the fence, I pulled the receiver back on the pistol and released it. I immediately heard his name, rank, serial number, and where he was stationed. Had I not stepped out in the open at this time, I think I would have heard much more.

Another one of our outings created another guard/officer confrontation. Our whole unit was together in a training area. There were buildings with beds in them for all of us. They decided there would be a different guard system. All the tanks were in one place. They made a list of tank crew members and decided each of us would watch the tanks one hour and awaken the next guy on the list. Glenn and I applied for the first two hours. We sat out there for two hours and talked. At the end of two hours, we woke up the next guy on the list.

I woke up about two in the morning to go to the bathroom. That involved walking by the guarded tanks, but there was no guard. Our tank was on the edge of the group, and I had to walk by it. It was a nice warm night. I was concerned about our tank being pilfered, so I bedded down on top of our tank. Just after dawn, a jeep with an officer and driver pulled up and woke me up, wanting to know why I was sleeping while I was on guard duty. When they found out why I was there and that I had witnesses, the matter was dropped.

What do you mean "shave"?

Sometimes the inspector general from Seventh Corps would do an unannounced or surprise inspection of the battalion. We were subjected to one of those surprise visits at the motor pool. Months before this, the motor pool sergeant, whose last name was Brown, decided G Company's vehicles needed to be spruced up. Each vehicle would get special individual attention. All platoons always had their vehicles parked in a line. It was the smallest vehicle first (jeeps) to biggest last in the line (tanks). Sergeant Brown had his staff start with the jeeps, which made a lot of sense when one understands the first jeep in the row is the one ridden in by the platoon leader, the highest-ranking person in the platoon. He also had them start with the Headquarters Platoon, which makes sense too. That first jeep was the company commander's vehicle. Sergeant Brown's staff had worked their way through all vehicles in headquarters, then through first and second platoon.

Two infantrymen discussing their last bath.

They made it all the way to the third platoon. They had completed the jeeps, the half-track, the APC, and one tank. Every piece of equipment in the motor pool now looked great, with the exception of tank G37, the one I drove. In comparison to the others, old G37 looked like it had no mother. Something else happened that day that was also an unusual error. I was the only tanker left. I stood behind my dirty-looking tank, watching the general and his entourage start their party at the other end of that line of squeaky-clean vehicles of all shapes and sizes. All of those vehicles had their assigned crews standing smartly at attention beside their vehicle.

The first sergeant, who chooses who has guard duty and who doesn't, had picked almost the whole eight-man squad who manned the two tanks in the third platoon. The two tank commanders were gone. They all had been given guard or other special duties that day.

The author with the captain's shoulder
holster and someone's Buick.

The inspector general's group consisted of three officers of lower rank who appeared to be his own yes-men. Walking with him, representing our company, was the company commander, three lieutenants, and First Sergeant Brown from the motor pool. As that group worked their way up the line toward me, I thought it looked as if there was going to be a public hanging or a scene from the OK Corral. Upon his arrival at our position, the general walked around the freshly painted tank first. He came to me as I was standing all alone by our two tanks, one of which was a mess. I think I did salute properly. He started by asking if that clean tank was my tank. When I answered no, he of course asked where the crew was. I told him I didn't know. That answer seemed to please the people who created this mess and were listening carefully to what was being said. He asked a few more questions which I tried to answer in a manner least threatening to our officers. After all, this was not my first conversation with an unhappy general!

The general moved from the clean tank to the remaining tank. He asked if it was mine. I responded as proudly as possible. He then asked if I was proud of it, and he got a no for an answer. I thought I sensed a lot of discomfort in the group in charge of G Company. I managed to work my way through the rest of the interrogation without blaming anyone or saying something really stupid. When that conversation ended, the general ordered the last tank to be looking like all the rest of the vehicles before *anyone* left the area. That order was not directed to me. It was directed to the group of officers and NCOs who represented G Company. The quick answer was to scrub it down with solvent. They made sure I was given men and materials needed to meet his orders.

The Czech/West German Border

Sign by the main entrance, twenty-two
miles from the observation post.

The whole Eleventh Cavalry Regiment shared two border camps. When a company pulled border duty, they were sent to a camp named Weiden Border Camp or one named Rotz Border Camp. Our headquarters and our barracks were at the same site until we returned to Regensburg. During my stay in Regensburg, we were sent one time to each of those villages. The camp at both sites seemed to be very near the town. Weiden was a little farther from the border, and seemed much like any other village I had experienced.

My pictures of Rotz Border Camp are all marked Christmas 1957. A visit to downtown Rotz had a much different feel about it. Except for the language they spoke and the fact they didn't wear cowboy boots, it felt as if I had been transported to the wild west of the United States as it was portrayed on TV at that time. It was very close to the border, and the populace seemed to be living in the moment. I am certain they knew that if there was conflict on the border, they would be the first casualties. I am aware there are unsavory civilian elements in the neighborhood of every army stopping place but Rotz seemed to have taken low morality to new levels. I made one trip downtown and never returned. I felt safer at the border.

Bunker, eight hundred yards from the border.
Private Fair sitting on the gas can.

The American side of the border between West Germany and communist nations was simply marked with a sign that said, "Attention—Fifty Meters to the Border." The entire border was fenced on the East German and Czechoslovakian frontier. The fences consisted of three rows of barbed wire that stretched the entire length of the border. The two outside rows of wire were about four feet tall. The center row was six to eight feet high and was supported with porcelain insulators indicating it was probably electrically charged. Their fences were often located from a few yards to hundreds of yards from the exact border. The fences sometimes had tunnels under them and had gates in them where roads passed. The gates had guards posted all the time, but the hundreds of watchtowers were not always manned. On some portions of the fence they plowed and raked a strip so it would be easy to see footprints if there were any people approaching the area at night. The responsibility of the Eleventh Cavalry, when they were at the border, was to establish a screen for other US tactical units by setting up defensive lines in our area if the need developed. The unspoken meaning of the words "need" or "threat" they were talking about was any action that could result in the beginning of WWIII. Their thought was that any threat in our region would come through Czechoslovakia. Keeping in mind that the city of Berlin at this time was like an open gate in a country that was totally divided by a fence, it should have surprised no one when on August 13, 1961, the Berlin Wall went up.

I was happy to be living back in Iowa when the wall was going up. The fence directed everyone to Berlin, and Berlin had been an open gate letting anyone out to the west. The site to which we were first assigned border duty was Weiden. There were three of us assigned to be at the border as a group. There were several groups of three assigned to different times and different sites. The phrase "at the border," as we used it, meant we were actually fifty yards or more away from it, and perhaps a quarter of a mile away from the border crossing. There was a small, rather ancient-looking, wooden bunker covered with tarpaper where we were posted.

The border is at the edge of the timber.

The bunker overlooked a length of the border, as well as the crossing where the highway that went to Pilsen crossed the border. In the bunker was a .30-caliber machine gun ready to fire and aimed at their border crossing. There was also a telescope in the bunker. Directly behind the bunker was a M55 armored personnel carrier (APC), whose purpose was to provide constant radio contact with headquarters. A jeep was parked by the bunker as well. The APC is the one powered by two GMC 6-cylinder engines, only one of which had a generator. That one engine ran all the time to assure constant radio contact. Some of the pictures show a person sitting on the five-gallon container used to bring gasoline to the border. The three of us at the site consisted of Sergeant Oxley, Private Fair from the infantry squad with his M1 rifle, and me.

We were the only army personnel authorized to be at the border site. We were to be notified in advance if anyone else was authorized. Typically, we would be on a normal schedule at the barracks on day one until late afternoon, when we would be briefed on the upcoming trip to the border. Next was the evening meal, and we would be transported to the border to relieve the ones there. This changing of the guard took place at eleven o'clock at night. We were expected to stay awake until we were relieved at eleven the next night. This duty revived my affair with quarter-pound Baby Ruth candy bars. We used the exhaust from the constantly running APC engine to heat coffee in canteen cups. Much coffee and candy thwarted going to sleep. Upon arriving at headquarters, debriefing, and finding some food, we became the untouchables. For all the next day we were not required to do anything but eat and sleep. The day after that, the cycle started over. We found a month of this to be exhausting. By the end of a month we didn't know what day it was or what time it was, and we really didn't care.

Alternative observation post position Site D – No roof, no radio, no place to warm the coffee.

A German Private First Class (PFC). They
were billeted in the same area as us.

In addition to our duties at the border, there was a scout squad
in a jeep, out patrolling border roads every day. It was not common
for us to cross paths with them. In addition, we would have visitors
from time to time. These visitors were two German customs police
and two German shepherd guard dogs. All four of them were a
living lesson in training and discipline. It was my understanding
that the German custom police with their dogs were responsible for
monitoring all the fence between East and West. This assignment
was accomplished on foot.

Trying to stay awake a few more hours.

In stark contrast to that discipline, one day we observed a US Army jeep on the highway. The stray jeep was approaching the gate at the border crossing on the highway to Pilsen. This crossing was manned by Czech military. Sergeant Oxley, the person in charge at our bunker, ordered me to take our jeep, and Private Fair with his M1 rifle, and see what was going on. For us this was near the end of our day's trip to the border. Our fatigues looked terrible, we hadn't shaved recently, and we hadn't slept for thirty hours. Fair came from the coal mining regions of Pennsylvania. He never looked like someone to be confronted not even when he was ready for inspection. When we got to the border crossing where a problem was located, Fair sat with his M1 across his lap with the muzzle pointing toward our visitors and a scowl on his face.

Our visitors turned out to be a second lieutenant with a driver. He was brand new to being an officer and brand new in Germany. He had been assigned to some unit many miles north of us. He had decided on his own authority to get a jeep and a driver and tour the countryside. This was no an approved US Army activity. The officer began to reprimand us for how we looked and for confronting an officer.

Fair looked more confrontive as I explained to the officer that on this ground he was not the one in charge, his rank was meaningless, and we were not playing games. We got their name, rank, and serial number. The lieutenant asked if I would take their picture in front of the sign marking the border crossing. That I was glad to do, because I knew this whole show would get to his commanding officer. When we debriefed in the morning and reported this incident, I was taken aback when the debriefing officer asked why I had not fired on them from the bunker. There were several good reasons for not firing live ammunition in the border crossing area. I really had no desire to be known as the guy who started WWIII. I also did not want to be there for that event if someone else started it. The army had another protocol, which was whenever you fired live ammo, you had to clean the weapon every day for three days after firing. I told the debriefing officer I didn't fire on them because I didn't want to have to go back out there and clean the weapon for three consecutive days.

Entrance to Rotz border camp.

Jere Probert

Our next trip to the border, we were sent to Rotz. It was winter, and neither my friend Glenn nor I were given border duty. Our responsibility was to make sure our tank would start and run every day. Glenn and I got to play a lot of shuffleboard on this assignment.

The barracks look like Arkansas with snow.

By the time February 1957 was on the calendar, Seventh Corps had come to the realization many of our vehicles were no longer trustworthy. When parts were needed, motor pool personnel would say, "There won't be replacement parts until Congress passes a new budget." That included things as common as batteries which were needed to start engines. What we called jumper cables in Iowa in army language became known as "slave cables." They were in high demand. Those cables moved around a lot. They were transferred from unit to unit. I think that was because they were easy to steal. Seventh Corps' solution for the condition of our tanks was to replace the M48 tanks currently in use in a tank battalion with new heavier models, and replace our badly worn M41s with the tanks formerly used by a heavy tank battalion in Northern Germany.

Christmas 1957.

A squad of us were randomly selected from the 11th ACR and placed on temporary duty (TDY) then sent to inspect our replacement tanks before they were transferred to us. Each of us had been issued TDY papers which in essence said it was okay for us to be where we were. One of the other soldiers in the TDY group and I decided we were bored and should go downtown for a while. We left the area very legitimately. When we left through the main gate, we asked the guards to inspect our TDY papers before they let us out. They had no problem with using the papers for a pass. Neither my newly found friend nor I were familiar with the German word *Fasching* or the American English phrase "Fat Tuesday." In either case, this evening was the Tuesday evening before Ash Wednesday. Since that day I have become aware that some in the United States celebrate that day. It is the last Tuesday before Ash Wednesday, when Lenten fasting starts.

As we wandered the streets of a German town, we were invited to join a group of eight or ten German citizens who were partying. We were in uniform so there was no question in their mind about who or what we represented. We were slightly literate in German, and they were slightly literate in English. They offered us beer served in a rather large glass boot that was passed around the table for everyone to drink. If anyone was concerned about germs in the beer, the main course ended that concern. Served with the beer was what my mother's family called "raw dog"—raw ground beef loaded with onions, pepper, and salt, and all in large quantities. I had managed to avoid eating or tasting the stuff at home for twenty-two years. I considered it to be a culinary nightmare. German-American relations got a little strained that evening as I tried to not eat the stuff, so I finally consumed a small amount with a large amount of bread. This group of Germans was comparatively well behaved all evening.

Visiting a former exchange student at Marburg.

When I made it home, I was told that a young Presbyterian pastor from a Church in my hometown happened to be teaching in Germany that same year as this happened to me. He ended up at a Fasching party in someone's home, and they were threatening to baptize him with German beer before he escaped the party.

At our party we had not been watching the time. The gates we left the camp through closed at midnight and suddenly it was a quarter to midnight. We explained our problem and one of the men offered to take us in his car. I think his car was a Messerschmitt. It had two wheels in front, one drive wheel in back, and a glass door that opened all the way across the front (and only) seat which comfortably seated three adults.

Glenn and the author back at Fort Skelly.

We had heard during the day that there was a break in the fence around the camp where a person could slip in or out unnoticed. We were told it was a small distance east of the main gate. Our Good Samaritan driver drove us directly to the main gate and stopped. It was past midnight now, so we, his passengers, said, "No, no!" He took off with us and went west rather than east. He seemed less friendly. He took us around the perimeter of the place. He got to the south where the married quarters and officer quarters were, stopped there, opened that glass door, and said, "*Roust.*" No knowledge of the German language was needed to comprehend the message. My friend and I walked the rest of the circle around that camp, found a place marked "Danger Impact Area," found the fence that was on the north side, found the hole in the fence, and were in our bunks by two in the morning. It could have been worse!

View from barracks at Weiden looking across
parade grounds toward German army billets.

My father started farming a family farm in 1933/34. The farm
was in the control of his uncle, who rented it to Dad on a fifty-fifty
crop-livestock contract. At that time, some parts of the United States
called it "sharecropping". Upon taking responsibility for the farm,
Dad hired a family to work for him. The hired man had worked
there continually from 1933 until I was in the army twenty-plus
years later. When I enlisted, it never entered my mind that he might
leave Dad after that many years of service to him.

He quit working there shortly after I left. My parents were
overworked and unable to find farm help. The army offered what
they called an "early release" to personnel who met the criteria of
need. Having seen one guy get an early release so he could try out for
a semipro baseball team, I had no moral qualms about applying for
an early release. If one met the requirements, the terms of the early
release were that you would get a release from active service ninety
days early. Since I had enlisted in the middle of August, I would be

home for most of the planting season if they approved my request. I met the requirements and was granted a release for May 1958.

Every German loves a tank; we always had spectators.

This time the ubiquitous "sorry about that" was because the company clerk forgot to process my papers after they were approved. I knew I was being sent to Fort Sheridan, Illinois, and I knew my release date, but I had no papers. We were within a couple of days of payday; so, in a case of bad judgment, I spent all my cash. The next day, as I was standing in line to turn in my winter gear, the company clerk hunted me up to tell me I was shipping out immediately. My friend, Glenn, fronted me twenty bucks for travel money. How ironic to have my army career begin and end with someone else's twenty dollars.

I was put in charge of two other guys, and we headed for Bremerhaven for another boat ride. The army had made arrangements to get me to Fort Sheridan. I didn't think the guys were nearly as sick on the return trip as they were on the way over.

February 6, 1958, moving out for war games.

My first action upon arrival at Fort Sheridan was to find the company office and apply for the money due me. This was money that I hadn't been able to access because the company office staff didn't process my papers on time and because of the travel schedule they had arranged. The first thing they did was tell me I wouldn't be released for three more days. The second thing I did was go back to the office and apply for a three-day leave. It seemed like everywhere I looked there were soldiers pushing lawnmowers. That was not how I planned to end my brief military career.

I took the duffel bag filled with my stuff, found a train headed for Milwaukee, Wisconsin, and joyfully boarded it. The train delivered me to southern Milwaukee and I headed for my brother's home in the northern part of town. I took my hundred pounds of duffel, and with the help of some patriotic (I was in uniform) bus drivers, I learned how to get transfers all the way across town. My brother, who had lived in Milwaukee a few years, claimed that being nice to their passengers was not ordinarily practiced by bus drivers in Milwaukee. The next day, in one of my brother Frank's cars, I almost had an uneventful trip home. It really was uneventful except for the speeding ticket right in front of the Catholic Church at the end of Main Street in McGregor, Iowa. I helped Dad for the days I had left in the army, drove my dad's car to Fort Sheridan, Illinois, picked up my release papers, and drove home.

The author's tank moving out February 6, 1958.

The man who handled our release ceremony stressed the fact that we were eligible for two things as a result of our service. The first eligibility, he said, was for recall back into the service any time in the next four years. The second was use of Veteran's medical facilities. When it all came to pass, I didn't get recalled and I have never been eligible for any VA benefits. I have no regrets about having the opportunity to spend those months in the uniform of the *army of the United States of America.*

Eleventh ACR ready to move out Allons!

Observation post.

Final Impressions:
★ Observations and ★
Afterthoughts

Regensburg, as previously stated, is/was in Bavaria. History books tell us that in WWII there was an assembly plant for Messerschmitt ME-109 or BF-109 airplanes in Regensburg. On August 17, 1943, the United States sent 146 B-17s to bomb the assembly plant. I have no data on the impact of the bombing, but twenty-four American planes were lost in the action. Historically, the region is predominately Roman Catholic. The city was proud of its churches in terms of how many, how large, and how elaborate they were. My memory is that there were more than three hundred churches in the city.

When traveling the rural areas, it was common to see small shrines alone in the fields. There were what appeared to be groups of farmers going from shrine to shrine and stopping at each one to pray. This was a spring-of-the-year activity and seemed like a good idea to me to be praying for the success of their crop year. The Danube River complex appeared to be a prospering addition to the city. It was also, justifiably, a matter of great pride for the citizens.

There was a young lady who decided to send me a gift while I was stationed in Regensburg. I have no memory of what the gift was, but it must have been slightly fragile. Apparently someone had told her to pack it in popcorn for protection. They forgot to tell her to pop the corn first. She must have paid shipping from Arlington, Iowa, to Regensburg, Germany, for at least five pounds of unpopped popcorn. I thought the only rational solution to this was to pop the corn. I got out the little stove from our field gear and a mess kit. One of the guys had KP that day, so he furnished the butter and we had freshly popped corn in the barracks that evening.

There was a man with the last name of Nichols who came from Baltimore City. He was a city guy who could have been the prototype for "The Fonz" of TV fame. Nichols did not know that corn could be popped in anything but one of those machines in a movie theater. He was fascinated by the whole process in the barracks that night.

I have a brother who has always strived for excellence in every endeavor. When he sent me a gift, he planned to send it in the best possible way. This was in the day when soda crackers were marketed retail in tin containers. The containers were the same size then as they are now. They held four rows of crackers about a foot high. He put his gift to me in the foot-high rectangular tin container and soldered the lid shut. This required the use of some equally creative tactical maneuvers to open the gift package.

A Soldier's Ultimate Embarrassment

During the good-weather months, our battalion held barracks inspection on Saturday. Sometimes it was followed by a battalion parade on the Fort Skelly parade grounds. If everyone was there for the parade, it would total nearly one thousand men in their dress uniforms, including spit-shined footwear, yellow scarves tucked around their necks, shined belt buckles, and buttons. It started with everyone on the grounds, including a drummer. One of the early activities was the presentation of the colors. This was implemented by a color guard. Every parade had a different color guard. There were three companies in the battalion. They were companies G, H, and I. A different company furnished the color guard for each parade. When a company had a second time to provide this group, they put different men on the color guard.

It was considered a rare privilege to be asked to be in that group. This was pomp and ceremony to the max. The guard was made up of four soldiers. There were two noncommissioned officers, one of whom carried the US flag, and the other carried the regimental flag. They were in the center of the group of four. Flanking them were two enlisted men, one on the left and one on the right. Those two were carrying their normal weapons.

When it became the time for G Company to provide the color guard, my friend Glenn and I were picked to be the enlisted men. When the day came, we got off to a good start. The battalion was called to attention, and the guard marched to the front to present the colors. One of the sergeants quietly counted cadence as we marched to the front. After the brief ceremony, we did an about-face and headed back.

The sergeant started calling cadence as he had done previously. The guy with the bass drum, clear at the other end of the grounds, decided it was his turn, so he started beating out his cadence on his drum. He didn't bother to start in sync with us. Here we were, a four-man guard representing G Company, in front of hundreds of guys standing at attention, and we were totally out of step with the drum. The sergeant called for us to change cadence, which is not that difficult. We successfully changed steps. The drummer made the same decision at the same time. He changed his cadence. Now we were not even close to being in step. We must have looked as if we were in a movie written and directed by the comedian Jerry Lewis. The sergeant finally gave the order to follow his call and forget the drum. Doing this, we did stay in step with each other as a group, but we quit trying to include the unknown drummer in the show. At least we didn't have to meet with any high-ranking officers after this experience.

Back in civilian life, if I were at a dance, I always made it clear that I couldn't stay in step with a bass drum. Some people become wallflowers for less reason than that.

My enlistment papers had clearly stated two years in the active reserves. Upon my release from active duty, they immediately began writing me reminding me of this commitment. Each time one of those letters arrived, Mother was convinced I was going to jail for some reason. She had no idea what the reason might be, but she was certain a reason existed. Fourteen months after my release, they sent me my orders. My two years of active reserves ended up being two weeks (ten days) with a reserve unit from Minnesota, training at Camp McCoy, Wisconsin. The discharge papers showed up in 1962. They became a framed treasure and hung on the wall.

Regensburg-area pictures.

A church in Cologne, a stop on our vacation trip.

A rural shrine.

Common rural scenes.

A German backyard

A view of Germany where it is flat

Documentation

The next seven pages are labeled "military record." Some of these pages were damaged in a fire where they were in Army storage in Saint Louis, Missouri.

INFORMAL INFORMATION REPLY DATE *March 29, 1985*

Re:

DATE OF INQUIRY	RECEIVED ON	ON BEHALF OF *PROBERT JERE G. 17477555*
REFERRED TO NPRC BY		

MILITARY SERVICE DOCUMENTS ARE EXTREMELY IMPORTANT. GUARD THEM CAREFULLY AGAINST LOSS OR DAMAGE. TO AVOID DELAYS IN OBTAINING THESE DOCUMENTS IN THE FUTURE, WE SUGGEST THAT YOU MAKE COPIES OF THE ENCLOSED DOCUMENTS.
THE REPLY TO THE INQUIRY WILL BE FOUND IN THE CHECKED ITEMS. IF IT IS NECESSARY TO WRITE TO US AGAIN CONCERNING THIS SUBJECT, PLEASE RETURN ALL PAPERS TO THIS CENTER.

[✓] Copies of requested military [✓] personnel [ ] medical records are attached.

[ ] The attached separation document may include the following information: Authority for separation, reason for separation, reenlistment eligibility code, and separation (SPN/SPD) Code. If you require a copy of the separation document that does not contain the above information, you may request a deleted copy from this center.

[✓] We regret some of the copies are of poor quality; however, they are the best copies obtainable.

[ ] The Privacy Act of 1974 does not permit the release of a social security number or other personal information to the public without the authorization of the veteran concerned. Therefore, personal identifying data relating to other persons have been deleted from the attached documents.

[ ] Military personnel, upon discharge from the Armed Forces, are issued discharge certificates. These certificates are prepared in the original only; therefore, copies cannot be furnished. The law does provide that upon presentation of satisfactory proof of loss (such as a signed statement), an honorably discharged veteran or the surviving spouse may be given a "certificate in lieu of lost or destroyed discharge." We are unable to issue a certificate in lieu to anyone other than as provided by law.

[ ] The document you have requested, DD Form 214, Report of Separation, was not used until Jan. 1, 1950. However, a similar form was used when you were separated. A copy of it is attached.

[ ] At the time you were separated, it was not the practice to issue a document which served as a report of separation.

[ ] The original Report of Separation was issued at the time of separation. Another original cannot be issued. The attached copy, however, will serve the same purpose as the original.

[ ] No Report of Separation was issued since you had no active service, or less than 90 days of active duty for training.

[ ] Your service record does not contain a copy of a Report of Separation, or its equivalent.

[✓] We are furnishing the attached Regional Form RG-6954, Certification of Military Service, *aloo* ~~in lieu of the requested document~~. This will verify your military service and may be used for any official purpose.

[ ] That portion of your request seeking Army service medals/awards has been referred to the U.S. Army Reserve Components Personnel and Administration Center, Attn: DARC-PSE-AW, 9700 Page Blvd., St. Louis, MO 63132. That office has jurisdiction over the issuance of Army medals and awards. Further correspondence on this subject should be addressed to that office.

[ ] The medical records you request: [ ] The documents you request pertaining to discharge: have been lent to the Veterans Administration and may be obtained from the VA office shown below.

[ ] Your Reenlistment Eligibility (RE) Code issued upon release from active duty on .... is ....

[ ] Your record of service in the .... indicates you were in a POW status from .... to ....

[ ] The reason and authority for your separation from active duty/discharge on .... is ....

NCPM *R.R.*

Jere Gene Probert
RR #1
Wadena, IA 52169

P. Powell
CAROLYN E. GRAHAM
for Chief, Records Reconstruction Branch
NATIONAL PERSONNEL RECORDS CENTER
(Military Personnel Records)
9700 Page Boulevard
St. Louis, MO 63132

GENERAL SERVICES ADMINISTRATION

RG-6920 (REV. 11/84)

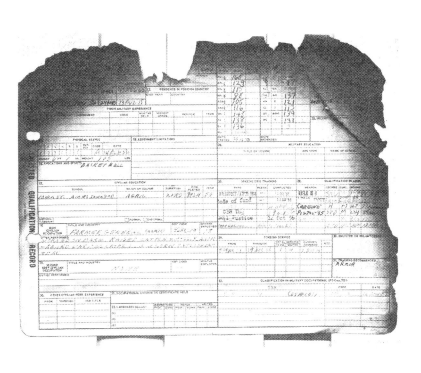

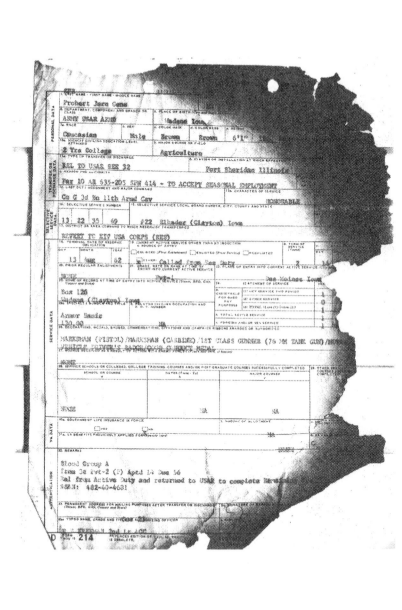

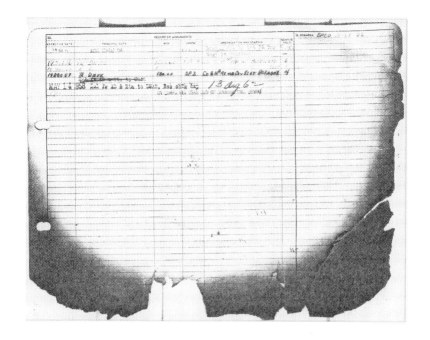

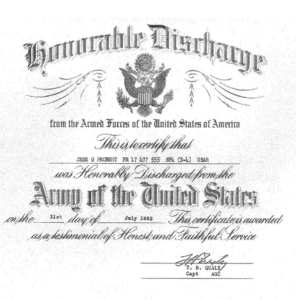

My old meal ticket.

Printed in the United States
By Bookmasters